TEACHING FOR ALL

DIFFERENTIATED INSTRUCTION STRATEGIES

DR. MINAKSHI BANSAL

DEDICATION

To all the students whose unique brilliance inspired this journey,

and to the educators who tirelessly dedicate themselves to nurturing every learner's potential.

Your passion fuels the flame of education,

and your commitment to differentiated instruction lights the way for a brighter future.

May this book be a guiding light on your path to creating inclusive and empowering classrooms

where every student thrives.

❧❧❧

Contents

Contents

Contents

Prayer

"Om Bhadram Karnebhih Shrinuyama Devah

Bhadram Pashyemakshabhiryajatrah

Sthirairangais Tushtuvamsastanubhih

Vyashema Devahitam Yadayuh

Svasti Na Indro Vriddhashravah

Svasti Nah Pusha Vishwavedah

Svasti Nastarkshyo Arishtanemih

Svasti No Brihaspatir Dadhatu

Om Shantih Shantih Shantih"

This mantra is a prayer for universal well-being, invoking the blessings of various deities for protection, health, and happiness. It emphasizes the importance of experiencing the auspicious through all senses and living a life aligned with divine purpose. The repetition of "Shantih" at the end signifies a deep desire for peace in the individual, the environment, and the universe at large. This mantra is often recited as a prayer for peace, prosperity, and the physical and spiritual well-being of all beings.

▷▷▷

About The Author

This book represents the culmination of extensive research and meticulous analysis, incorporating a diverse range of sources, including numerous books, scholarly studies, and personal experiences. Additionally, I have scoured various websites to gather relevant information and data essential for the compilation of this work. I have taken every precaution to ensure the accuracy of the information presented and have diligently cited all sources to acknowledge their contributions.

From her earliest days, Minakshi was distinguished by an insatiable appetite for reading. Her literary universe was inhabited by characters and narratives that spanned ethical tales, motivational and inspirational stories, and the mythic parables imbued with life lessons. This voracious reading habit was not merely for personal edification but was driven by a desire to distill and disseminate the essence of these narratives to foster the development of students and peers alike. She was particularly captivated by the lives and teachings of historical figures and spiritual leaders such as Adi Shankaracharya, Swami Vivekananda, Dr. APJ Abdul Kalam, Mahamana Pandit Madan Mohan Malviya, Mahatma Gandhi, Sardar Vallabhai Patel, and Vinoba Bhave, among others. Their philosophies and life stories fueled her ambition to embody their ideals of resilience, selflessness, and relentless pursuit of knowledge.

Dr. Minakshi's academic and practical engagement with psychology has been equally noteworthy. As a research scholar, her focus has been on exploring the intricate tapestry of the human psyche, aiming to unlock the potential for psychological well-being and societal harmony. Her scholarly work is complemented by her active involvement in social work, where she employs her academic insights to make tangible differences in the lives of the underprivileged. Her endeavours in social work are characterized by an innovative approach that combines traditional wisdom with contemporary psychological practices to address the multifaceted challenges faced by these communities.

Her artistic talents, another facet of her diverse capabilities, are not merely a personal passion but also serve as a medium through which she communicates and connects with others. Her art, rich in symbolism and emotional depth, reflects her philosophical inquiries and social concerns, offering viewers a glimpse into the breadth of her intellect and the depth of her compassion.

In addition to her contributions to the arts and social sciences, Dr. Minakshi has embraced the healing arts of Pranic Healing, mastering the techniques developed by Master Choa Kok Sui. This practice, which focuses on the manipulation of Prana or life energy to heal the body and aura, has been both a personal journey of discovery and a means through which she extends her healing touch to others. Her proficiency in Pranic Healing is complemented by her advocacy and teaching of various forms of meditation aimed at rejuvenation, personal betterment, and the cultivation of harmony within individuals and communities alike.

Dr. Minakshi's life is a narrative of relentless pursuit, not just of personal achievement but of the upliftment and empowerment of society at large. Her diverse interests and talents—spanning the arts, literature, psychology, and the healing practices—converge on a singular path of service. She embodies the spirit of the luminaries who inspired her, channelling their legacy through her actions and teachings. Through her books, art, and social initiatives, she continues to inspire a new generation to embark on their own journeys of self-discovery, resilience, and altruism.

Her commitment to social betterment, particularly her focus on uplifting underprivileged children, reflects a deep understanding of the transformative potential of education and personal development. By integrating her knowledge of psychology, her artistic sensibilities, and her healing practices, Dr. Bansal has developed a holistic approach to social work that addresses both the immediate needs and the long-term well-being of the communities she serves.

As an author, Dr. Minakshi's writings offer a blend of inspirational insights, practical wisdom, and reflective contemplations drawn from her extensive reading and life experiences. Her books serve as a guide for those seeking to navigate the complexities of life with grace, resilience, and purpose. Through her narratives, she extends an invitation to her readers to explore the depths of their own potential and to contribute meaningfully to the collective well-being of society.

In Dr. Minakshi Bansal, we find a remarkable synthesis of the artist, the scholar, the healer, and the social activist. Her life's work stands as a beacon of hope and a source of inspiration for individuals seeking to make a difference in the world. Her story is a compelling reminder of the power of individual action, rooted in compassion and driven by a profound commitment to the betterment of humanity. Dr. Minakshi's legacy is not just in the tangible outcomes of her efforts but in the enduring spirit of inquiry, empathy, and service that she embodies.

ᐁᐁᐁ

Preface

As I embarked on my journey as an educator, I was filled with idealism and a deep-seated belief in the transformative power of education. I envisioned a classroom where every student, regardless of their background or abilities, would feel valued, challenged, and empowered to reach their full potential. However, as I stepped into the real world of teaching, I quickly realized that the traditional, one-size-fits-all approach to instruction was falling short. Many of my students were struggling to keep up, while others were bored and unchallenged. I knew there had to be a better way.

This realization sparked my interest in differentiated instruction, a student-centered approach that tailors teaching to the diverse needs of all learners. I began to devour books and articles on the subject, attend workshops and conferences, and experiment with different strategies in my own classroom. The more I learned, the more convinced I became that differentiated instruction was the key to unlocking the full potential of every student.

This book, "Teaching for All," is the culmination of my years of research, reflection, and practice. It is a comprehensive guide to differentiated instruction, offering practical strategies and tools that educators can use to create inclusive and engaging learning environments where every student can thrive. Whether you are a novice teacher just starting your journey or a seasoned veteran seeking new ideas, this book will provide you with the knowledge and inspiration you need to transform your classroom into a place where all students feel valued, challenged, and empowered.

In this book, I delve into the core principles of differentiated instruction, exploring why it is essential for today's diverse learners and how it can be implemented effectively in the classroom. I share a wealth of strategies for differentiating content, process, product, and the learning environment, providing concrete examples and case studies to illustrate how these strategies can be applied in real-world settings.

I also address some of the common challenges that educators face when implementing differentiated instruction, offering practical solutions and tips for overcoming these obstacles. I believe that all teachers, regardless of their experience or expertise, can successfully implement differentiated instruction with the right support and resources.

This book is not just a theoretical guide; it is a practical handbook filled with actionable strategies and real-world examples. I have drawn from my own experiences as a teacher, as well as the experiences of countless other educators who have embraced differentiated instruction. I have also incorporated the latest research and insights from the field of education, ensuring that this book is both relevant and up-to-date.

My hope is that this book will inspire and empower educators to embrace differentiated instruction and transform their classrooms into vibrant learning communities where all students can reach their full potential. I believe that every student deserves an education that is tailored to their individual needs and interests, and I am confident that differentiated instruction is the key to achieving this goal.

I invite you to join me on this journey of discovery and transformation. As you read this book, I encourage you to reflect on your own teaching practices, experiment with new strategies, and embrace the challenges and rewards of differentiated instruction. Together, we can create a brighter future for all learners.

This book is not just for teachers; it is for anyone who cares about education and the future of our children. Whether you are a parent, administrator, policymaker, or simply a concerned citizen, I believe that this book will provide you with valuable insights into the power of differentiated instruction and its potential to transform our educational system.

I would like to express my sincere gratitude to all the students, teachers, colleagues, and mentors who have inspired and supported me throughout my career. Your dedication to education and your passion for learning have been a constant source of inspiration. I am also grateful to my family and friends for their unwavering support and encouragement.

Finally, I would like to dedicate this book to all the students who have taught me so much about the power of learning. You are the reason I became a teacher, and you are the reason I continue to strive for excellence in my profession. I hope that this book will help you achieve your dreams and reach your full potential.

Dr. Minakshi Bansal
Social Activist
Ahmedabad, Gujarat, Bharat

ONE

Understanding Differentiated Instruction: Tailoring Teaching to Every Student

In the vibrant tapestry of a classroom, each student is a unique thread, woven with diverse strengths, challenges, interests, and learning styles. Differentiated instruction is the art of tailoring teaching to honor this individuality, recognizing that one size does not fit all when it comes to learning. It's a student-centered approach that empowers educators to create inclusive and engaging learning environments where every student can thrive.

At its core, differentiated instruction is not about creating separate lessons for each student; rather, it's about providing a flexible framework that can adapt to the needs of all learners. It's a shift in mindset from teaching to a hypothetical "average" student to recognizing and celebrating the diverse needs within a classroom. This means understanding that students learn at different paces, have varying interests, and possess unique ways of processing and demonstrating their understanding.

Imagine a classroom where some students grasp concepts quickly while others need more time and support. Some learners are visual learners, thriving with images and diagrams, while others prefer hands-on activities or auditory explanations. Some are intrinsically motivated by their curiosity, while others need external encouragement and structure. Differentiated instruction acknowledges these differences and seeks to provide multiple pathways to learning.

The first step in differentiating instruction is truly knowing your students. This involves ongoing assessment and observation to gather information about their readiness levels, interests, and learning profiles. Formal assessments, such as pre-tests and standardized tests, can provide valuable data, but informal observations and conversations with students are equally important. By understanding each student's strengths and areas for growth, teachers can begin to tailor their instruction accordingly.

Differentiation can take many forms. One way is by differentiating content, which means adjusting the complexity or depth of the material to meet individual needs. For instance, some students may be ready to tackle advanced concepts, while others might benefit from additional scaffolding and support. Teachers can provide different texts or resources, offer varying levels of complexity within a task, or use tiered assignments that allow students to choose the level of challenge that suits them.

Differentiating the learning process is another crucial aspect. This involves providing students with different ways to access and engage with the content. Some learners might thrive in collaborative groups, while others prefer independent work. Some might need more explicit instruction and guided practice, while others are ready for more open-ended inquiry. Teachers can use various instructional strategies, such as hands-on activities, visual aids, graphic organizers, and technology tools, to cater to different learning styles.

Differentiation also extends to how students demonstrate their learning. Some learners excel at written assignments, while others are more expressive through oral presentations or artistic projects. Providing a variety of assessment options allows students to showcase their understanding in ways that best align with their strengths. This could involve offering choices in how students demonstrate their knowledge, such as creating a video, writing a report, or designing a model.

The physical learning environment also plays a role in differentiation. Creating a welcoming and supportive classroom where all students feel valued and respected is essential. This involves providing flexible seating arrangements, quiet corners for individual work, and collaborative spaces for group projects. Incorporating visual cues, such as anchor charts and word walls, can also aid learning for different students.

Technology can be a powerful tool for differentiation. Educational software, online resources, and assistive technologies can provide personalized learning experiences tailored to individual needs. Adaptive learning platforms, for example, can adjust the content and pace of instruction based on student performance, ensuring that each learner receives the appropriate level of challenge and support.

Differentiating instruction is an ongoing process that requires creativity, flexibility, and a commitment to meeting the needs of all students. It's about fostering a love of learning, empowering students to take ownership of their education, and creating a classroom where everyone feels seen, heard, and valued. While it may seem daunting at first, the rewards of differentiated instruction are immeasurable. By embracing this student-centered approach, educators can unlock the full potential of every learner and create a more equitable and inclusive learning environment for all.

ᗣᗣᗣ

Every student is a universe of potential waiting to be unlocked. Differentiated instruction is the key that opens the door to their unique brilliance. Let's celebrate diversity and empower every learner to shine.

TWO
WHY DIFFERENTIATE?: THE BENEFITS FOR STUDENTS AND TEACHERS

The landscape of education is ever-evolving, and the one-size-fits-all approach to teaching is increasingly recognized as inadequate for meeting the diverse needs of today's students. Differentiated instruction, a student-centered approach that tailors teaching to individual learners, is emerging as a powerful tool to transform classrooms into inclusive and engaging learning environments. The benefits of differentiated instruction extend to both students and teachers, creating a ripple effect that positively impacts the entire educational ecosystem.

For students, differentiated instruction is a game-changer. It recognizes that each learner is unique, with their own set of strengths, challenges, interests, and learning styles. By acknowledging and honoring this diversity, differentiated instruction empowers students to reach their full potential. When lessons are tailored to their specific needs, students are more likely to be engaged and motivated, as they can connect with the material in ways that resonate with them. This increased engagement not only leads to deeper understanding but also fosters a lifelong love of learning.

Differentiated instruction also helps students develop essential 21st-century skills, such as critical thinking, problem-solving, collaboration, and communication. By providing opportunities for choice and autonomy, differentiated instruction encourages students to take ownership of their learning. They become active participants in the educational process, setting goals, making decisions, and evaluating their progress. This sense of ownership not only enhances their academic performance but also prepares them for success in the real world, where adaptability and self-direction are highly valued.

Moreover, differentiated instruction promotes a more inclusive classroom environment. When students feel seen, heard, and understood, they are more likely to feel a sense of belonging and connection to their school community. This can be particularly beneficial for students who have traditionally been marginalized or underserved, such as those with learning differences, English language learners, or gifted learners. Differentiated instruction provides these students with the support and challenges they need to thrive, ensuring that they are not left behind or held back.

The benefits of differentiated instruction are not limited to students; teachers also reap significant rewards from this approach. By differentiating their instruction, teachers can create more engaging and effective learning experiences for all students. They can witness firsthand the joy of seeing students discover their passions, overcome challenges, and achieve their goals. This can be immensely gratifying and can reignite a teacher's passion for their profession.

Differentiated instruction also allows teachers to better understand their students as individuals. By observing how students respond to different instructional strategies, teachers can gain valuable insights into their learning styles, strengths, and areas for growth. This knowledge can then inform future lesson planning and instruction, creating a continuous cycle of improvement.

Furthermore, differentiated instruction can help teachers address the diverse needs of their students more effectively. In today's classrooms, teachers are faced with the challenge of educating students with a wide range of abilities and backgrounds. Differentiated instruction provides a framework for meeting this challenge, allowing teachers to tailor their instruction to the specific needs of each student, while still ensuring that all learners are working towards the same academic standards.

While differentiated instruction offers numerous benefits, it is not without its challenges. It requires careful planning, ongoing assessment, and a willingness to experiment with different approaches. Teachers may need to invest additional time and effort in developing differentiated lessons and materials. However, the long-term benefits for both students and teachers far outweigh the initial investment.

In conclusion, differentiated instruction is a powerful tool that can transform classrooms into vibrant learning communities where every student can thrive. By tailoring teaching to individual learners, differentiated instruction empowers students to reach their full potential, fosters essential 21st-century skills, and promotes a more inclusive learning environment. For teachers, differentiated instruction provides a more engaging and effective way to teach, a deeper understanding of their students, and the ability to address the diverse needs of their classrooms. While it may present some challenges, the rewards of differentiated instruction are immeasurable. By embracing this student-centered approach, educators can unlock the full potential of every learner and create a more equitable and inclusive educational system for all.

᭓᭓᭓

In the symphony of learning, each student plays a different instrument. Differentiated instruction is the conductor, harmonizing their individual melodies into a beautiful composition. Let's create a classroom where every voice is heard and valued.

THREE

KNOWING YOUR STUDENTS: ASSESSMENT AND OBSERVATION STRATEGIES

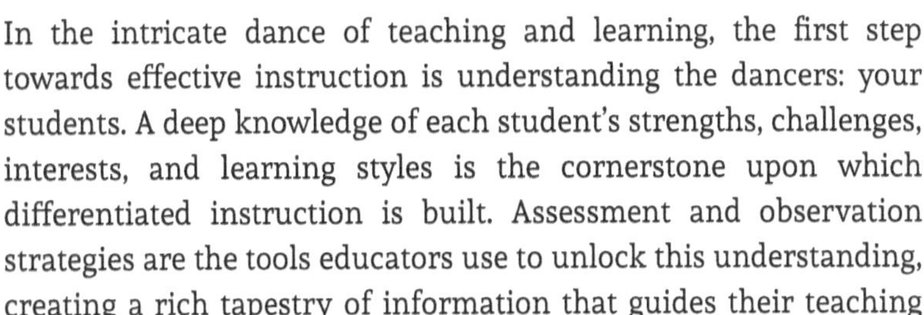

In the intricate dance of teaching and learning, the first step towards effective instruction is understanding the dancers: your students. A deep knowledge of each student's strengths, challenges, interests, and learning styles is the cornerstone upon which differentiated instruction is built. Assessment and observation strategies are the tools educators use to unlock this understanding, creating a rich tapestry of information that guides their teaching practices.

Assessment, in the context of differentiated instruction, goes beyond simply measuring student achievement. It's a multifaceted process that encompasses a wide range of techniques designed to gather information about students' readiness levels, learning profiles, and interests. This information, in turn, informs instructional decisions, allowing teachers to tailor their teaching to meet the diverse needs of their students.

Formal assessments, such as standardized tests, quizzes, and unit exams, provide valuable quantitative data about student performance. These assessments can help identify students who may need additional support or those who are ready for more challenging material. However, it's important to remember that formal assessments only capture a snapshot of student learning and may not fully reflect their abilities or potential.

Informal assessments, on the other hand, offer a more holistic view of student learning. These assessments can take many forms, such as observations, anecdotal notes, conversations with students, and analysis of student work samples. They provide a window into students' thinking processes, problem-solving strategies, and areas of interest. Informal assessments can be particularly useful for identifying students' strengths and challenges that may not be apparent in formal testing situations.

Observations are a powerful tool for gathering information about student learning. By carefully observing students during class activities, group work, and independent tasks, teachers can gain insights into their engagement levels, social interactions, and preferred learning styles. Observations can also reveal misconceptions or gaps in understanding that may need to be addressed.

Anecdotal notes are brief, informal records of specific student behaviors or interactions. These notes can capture moments of insight or highlight areas where students may need additional support. They can be used to track student progress over time and inform instructional decisions.

Conversations with students provide a valuable opportunity for teachers to get to know their students on a personal level. By asking open-ended questions, actively listening to student responses, and engaging in meaningful dialogue, teachers can learn about their students' interests, aspirations, and challenges. These conversations can also help build rapport and trust, creating a positive learning environment where students feel comfortable taking risks and asking for help.

Analysis of student work samples, such as essays, projects, and presentations, can reveal a wealth of information about their understanding of the material, their critical thinking skills, and their creativity. By carefully examining student work, teachers can identify areas where students excel and areas where they may need additional instruction or feedback.

The data gathered through assessments and observations can be used to create student profiles that outline their strengths, challenges, interests, and learning styles. These profiles can then be used to inform instructional decisions, such as grouping students for differentiated activities, selecting appropriate materials and resources, and designing assessments that cater to diverse learning needs.

It's important to note that assessment and observation are not one-time events but rather ongoing processes. Teachers need to continuously monitor student progress and adjust their instruction accordingly. By regularly checking for understanding, providing feedback, and celebrating student successes, teachers can create a dynamic learning environment where all students feel supported and challenged to reach their full potential.

In conclusion, knowing your students is the foundation of differentiated instruction. By employing a variety of assessment and observation strategies, teachers can gain a deep understanding of each student's unique needs and tailor their teaching accordingly. This student-centered approach not only enhances student engagement and achievement but also fosters a more inclusive and equitable learning environment where all students can thrive.

❦❦❦

The classroom is not a factory producing identical products; it's a garden where diverse flowers bloom. Differentiated instruction is the gardener, nurturing each plant's unique needs. Let's cultivate a learning environment where every student thrives.

FOUR

DIFFERENTIATING CONTENT: ADAPTING WHAT STUDENTS LEARN

In the vibrant tapestry of a differentiated classroom, adapting the content that students learn is a fundamental pillar. Just as a skilled tailor adjusts a garment to fit each individual's unique physique, a differentiated approach to content ensures that the educational material aligns with the diverse learning needs and abilities of all students. This involves thoughtfully selecting, modifying, and presenting content in ways that engage, challenge, and support every learner on their educational journey.

At its core, differentiating content recognizes that a one-size-fits-all approach to curriculum falls short in meeting the diverse needs of today's students. Some students might be ready to delve into complex concepts, while others require more foundational support. Some learners thrive with abstract ideas, while others grasp information more readily through concrete examples. Some are intrinsically motivated by intellectual curiosity, while others need external scaffolding and encouragement. By acknowledging these differences, educators can create learning experiences that resonate with each student's individual learning profile.

One effective strategy for differentiating content is tiered instruction. This involves creating multiple levels of complexity within a single topic or unit of study. Each tier presents the same essential concepts but with varying degrees of depth and challenge. For instance, in a science lesson on the solar system, students might be offered three tiers: one focusing on basic planetary facts, another delving into the intricacies of planetary orbits and composition, and a third exploring advanced concepts such as astrophysics. This approach allows students to work at a level that is both challenging and attainable, promoting optimal learning and growth.

Another way to differentiate content is through flexible grouping. This involves strategically grouping students based on their readiness levels, interests, or learning styles. For example, in a language arts class, students might be grouped by reading level for a literature circle discussion, or by interest for a research project. Flexible grouping allows teachers to tailor instruction to the specific needs of each group, providing targeted support and enrichment as needed.

Choice boards are another powerful tool for differentiating content. These visual organizers present students with a variety of options for learning activities related to a particular topic. For instance, in a social studies unit on ancient civilizations, a choice board might offer options such as reading a historical fiction novel, creating a timeline of key events, building a model of a famous landmark, or writing a letter from the perspective of a historical figure. This approach empowers students to choose activities that align with their interests and learning preferences, fostering a sense of ownership and engagement in their learning.

Technology can also play a pivotal role in differentiating content. Digital resources, such as online textbooks, interactive simulations, and educational videos, can offer students multiple ways to access and engage with information. Adaptive learning platforms can personalize learning experiences based on individual student performance, providing tailored content and feedback. Additionally, assistive technologies can support students with disabilities, ensuring that all learners have equal access to the curriculum.

Differentiated content goes beyond simply adjusting the level of difficulty. It involves providing diverse perspectives, offering multiple modalities of learning, and creating opportunities for student choice and voice. For example, in a history lesson on the civil rights movement, students might explore primary sources such as letters, speeches, and photographs, alongside secondary sources such as textbooks and documentaries. They might also engage in debates, role-playing activities, or creative projects that allow them to express their understanding in unique ways.

Ultimately, differentiating content is about creating a rich and varied learning landscape that caters to the diverse needs and interests of all students. It's about fostering a love of learning by presenting content in ways that are engaging, relevant, and meaningful. By embracing this student-centered approach, educators can unlock the full potential of every learner, ensuring that all students have the opportunity to succeed and thrive.

ppp

One size does not fit all in education. Differentiated instruction is the tailor, customizing learning experiences to fit each student's unique measurements. Let's empower learners to reach their full potential by meeting them where they are.

FIVE

DIFFERENTIATING PROCESS: ADAPTING HOW STUDENTS LEARN

Within the dynamic landscape of differentiated instruction, adapting how students learn—differentiating process—is a cornerstone of effective teaching. It recognizes that learners engage with and process information in diverse ways, requiring educators to provide a multitude of avenues for students to grasp, internalize, and apply knowledge.

By offering varied instructional approaches, educators empower students to leverage their unique strengths and preferences, fostering a deeper understanding of the subject matter and promoting a lifelong love of learning.

At its heart, differentiating process acknowledges that learning is not a one-size-fits-all endeavor. Some students excel in structured, teacher-led environments, while others thrive with independent exploration. Some learners prefer to collaborate and share ideas with peers, while others prefer to work alone and reflect on their own. Some grasp concepts quickly through auditory explanations, while others require visual representations or hands-on activities.

By understanding these diverse learning styles and preferences, educators can create a dynamic learning environment where each student can find their own path to success.

One powerful strategy for differentiating process is providing students with choice. This could involve offering a variety of learning activities related to a particular topic, allowing students to select the ones that resonate with their interests and learning styles.

For example, in a unit on the American Revolution, students might choose to research and present on a specific historical figure, write a creative story from the perspective of a Revolutionary War soldier, or participate in a debate on the causes of the conflict. By allowing students to make choices, educators foster a sense of ownership and agency in their learning, increasing their engagement and motivation.

Another way to differentiate process is by incorporating multiple modalities of learning. This means presenting information in various formats, such as auditory, visual, and kinesthetic. For instance, in a science lesson on the human body, students might listen to a lecture, watch a video, dissect a model, or create a diagram to illustrate their understanding. By appealing to different senses and learning styles, educators can ensure that all students have access to the information and can process it in ways that make sense to them.

Scaffolding is another crucial element of differentiating process. This involves providing students with varying levels of support based on their individual needs. For instance, some students might need more explicit instruction and guided practice, while others are ready for more independent exploration and discovery. Scaffolding can be provided through graphic organizers, modeling, prompts, sentence starters, and other tools that help students access and process information at their own pace.

Technology can also be a valuable tool for differentiating process. Educational software, online resources, and assistive technologies can provide personalized learning experiences tailored to individual needs. Adaptive learning platforms, for example, can adjust the pace and content of instruction based on student performance, ensuring that each learner is challenged and supported appropriately. Additionally, virtual reality and augmented reality tools can create immersive learning experiences that cater to different learning styles.

Incorporating collaborative learning activities is another effective way to differentiate process. By working together in small groups or pairs, students can learn from each other, share ideas, and build on each other's strengths. Collaborative learning can also promote social and emotional development, as students learn to communicate effectively, negotiate, and resolve conflicts.

Differentiated process goes beyond simply providing different learning activities. It involves creating a learning environment that is flexible, responsive, and inclusive. It means fostering a culture of respect for individual differences, where all students feel valued and supported in their learning journeys. It means providing opportunities for students to explore their interests, express their creativity, and develop their critical thinking skills.

Ultimately, differentiating process is about empowering students to become independent, self-directed learners. By providing them with the tools, strategies, and support they need to learn in ways that work best for them, educators can unlock the full potential of every learner.

When students are actively engaged in the learning process, they are more likely to develop a deep understanding of the subject matter, retain information longer, and apply their knowledge in new and creative ways.

ᗡᗡᗡ

Learning is not a race to the finish line; it's a journey of exploration and discovery. Differentiated instruction is the compass, guiding students along their individual paths. Let's create a classroom where every student's journey is valued.

SIX

DIFFERENTIATING PRODUCT: ADAPTING HOW STUDENTS DEMONSTRATE LEARNING

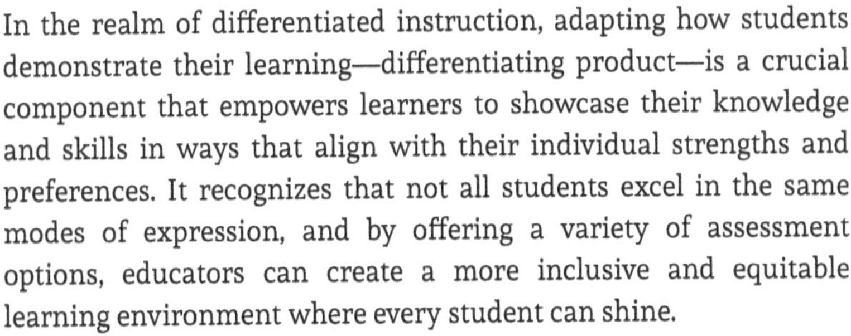

In the realm of differentiated instruction, adapting how students demonstrate their learning—differentiating product—is a crucial component that empowers learners to showcase their knowledge and skills in ways that align with their individual strengths and preferences. It recognizes that not all students excel in the same modes of expression, and by offering a variety of assessment options, educators can create a more inclusive and equitable learning environment where every student can shine.

Traditional assessments, such as standardized tests and written essays, often privilege certain types of learners, leaving others feeling discouraged or undervalued. Differentiating product breaks free from this mold, allowing students to express their understanding in diverse and creative ways. This not only enhances student engagement and motivation but also provides a more comprehensive picture of their learning.

One way to differentiate product is by offering students choice in how they demonstrate their knowledge. This could involve allowing them to choose between various formats, such as written reports, oral presentations, visual projects, artistic creations, or multimedia presentations. For example, in a history class, students might have the option to write a traditional essay, create a historical documentary, design a museum exhibit, or perform a skit depicting a key event. By providing choice, educators tap into students' intrinsic motivation and encourage them to take ownership of their learning.

Another approach to differentiating product is by varying the level of complexity or challenge. This can be achieved by offering tiered assignments that allow students to choose the level of difficulty that suits their readiness and skills. For instance, in a science unit on the human body, students might be offered three different project options: one focusing on basic anatomy, another delving into the functions of specific organs, and a third exploring advanced concepts such as physiology and disease. This tiered approach ensures that all students are challenged and engaged, regardless of their prior knowledge or skill level.

Incorporating student interests into product assignments is another effective way to differentiate. When students are passionate about a topic, they are more likely to invest time and effort into their work, leading to deeper learning and greater satisfaction. For example, in a literature class, students might be allowed to choose a book that aligns with their personal interests and create a product that reflects their unique interpretation of the text. This could involve writing a critical analysis, composing a song inspired by the story, or designing a book cover that captures the essence of the narrative.

Technology can also be a powerful tool for differentiating product. Digital tools and platforms offer a vast array of possibilities for students to express their creativity and showcase their learning. They can create multimedia presentations, design websites, code interactive games, or produce podcasts. By leveraging technology, educators can not only cater to different learning styles but also prepare students for the digital age.

Differentiated product also involves providing students with clear expectations and criteria for success. Rubrics can be particularly helpful in this regard, outlining the specific skills and knowledge that students need to demonstrate. Rubrics can also be differentiated to accommodate different levels of readiness and skill, ensuring that all students have a fair and equitable opportunity to succeed.

It's important to note that differentiating product is not about lowering standards or giving some students an easier path to success. Rather, it's about providing all students with the opportunity to demonstrate their learning in ways that are meaningful and authentic to them. When students are allowed to express themselves in ways that align with their strengths and interests, they are more likely to take pride in their work, develop a sense of accomplishment, and achieve their full potential.

In conclusion, differentiating product is a cornerstone of effective differentiated instruction. By offering a variety of assessment options, tailoring assignments to individual needs and interests, and providing clear expectations and criteria for success, educators can create a more inclusive and equitable learning environment where every student can thrive. When students are empowered to showcase their learning in ways that are meaningful and authentic to them, they not only achieve academic success but also develop the critical thinking, creativity, and communication skills that are essential for success in the 21st century.

❧❧❧

The classroom is a canvas, and every student is an artist. Differentiated instruction is the palette, providing a rich array of colors and tools for self-expression. Let's inspire creativity and empower students to paint their own masterpieces.

SEVEN

DIFFERENTIATING THE LEARNING ENVIRONMENT: CREATING A SUPPORTIVE CLASSROOM

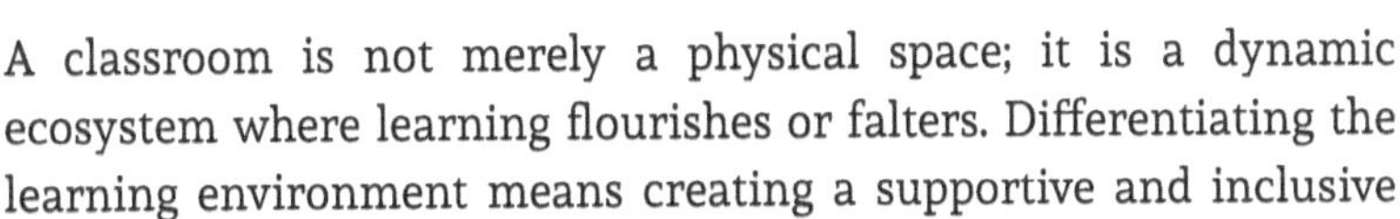

A classroom is not merely a physical space; it is a dynamic ecosystem where learning flourishes or falters. Differentiating the learning environment means creating a supportive and inclusive space that caters to the diverse needs of all students.

It involves thoughtful consideration of the physical layout, classroom culture, and instructional practices, all with the aim of fostering a sense of belonging, engagement, and empowerment for every learner.

The physical layout of a classroom can significantly impact student learning. Traditional rows of desks facing a teacher-centered front of the room may not be conducive to collaboration or active learning.

A differentiated learning environment offers a variety of flexible seating arrangements, such as small group tables, individual workspaces, and comfortable reading nooks. This allows students to choose the environment that best suits their learning preferences and tasks.

The classroom should also be visually stimulating and inviting. Posters, artwork, and student work can create a sense of pride and ownership. Natural light, plants, and calming colors can promote a positive and focused atmosphere. Noise levels should be managed to minimize distractions and create a peaceful learning environment for those who need it.

Beyond the physical space, the classroom culture plays a crucial role in differentiating the learning environment. A supportive classroom culture values diversity, fosters respect, and encourages collaboration. It celebrates individual differences and provides a safe space for students to express themselves, take risks, and make mistakes.

Establishing clear expectations and routines helps students feel secure and focused. Positive reinforcement and recognition of effort and progress create a sense of accomplishment and motivation. Opportunities for student choice and autonomy empower learners to take ownership of their education and develop self-regulation skills.

A differentiated learning environment also promotes a sense of community and belonging. Students should feel connected to their classmates and teacher, fostering a sense of camaraderie and mutual support. Collaborative learning activities, such as group projects and peer feedback sessions, encourage students to work together, share ideas, and learn from each other.

The teacher's role in differentiating the learning environment is paramount. They are not just instructors but facilitators, mentors, and guides.

They create a welcoming and inclusive atmosphere, build positive relationships with students, and model respect for diversity. They set high expectations for all learners while providing the necessary support to help them reach their full potential.

Differentiated instruction is not just about adapting content and process; it's also about differentiating assessment. Instead of relying solely on standardized tests, a differentiated classroom offers a variety of assessment options, such as performance tasks, portfolios, and self-assessments. This allows students to demonstrate their learning in ways that best suit their strengths and preferences.

Technology can also be a powerful tool for differentiating the learning environment. Digital resources, such as online textbooks, interactive simulations, and educational games, can cater to diverse learning styles and interests. Assistive technologies, such as screen readers and text-to-speech software, can make learning more accessible for students with disabilities.

It's important to note that differentiating the learning environment is an ongoing process. Teachers need to continuously monitor student engagement and well-being, adjusting their practices as needed. They should seek feedback from students, parents, and colleagues to ensure that the learning environment is meeting the needs of all learners.

In conclusion, differentiating the learning environment is a holistic approach that encompasses the physical space, classroom culture, instructional practices, and assessment strategies. It's about creating a supportive and inclusive space where all students feel valued, respected, and empowered to learn.

By thoughtfully considering the needs of their diverse learners, educators can create a classroom environment that truly fosters growth, creativity, and a lifelong love of learning.

❧❧❧

Assessment is not a judgment; it's a flashlight illuminating the path ahead. Differentiated assessment is the map, revealing each student's unique strengths and areas for growth. Let's guide learners towards success by providing them with personalized feedback.

EIGHT

FLEXIBLE GROUPING: STRATEGIES FOR COLLABORATIVE LEARNING

In the ever-evolving landscape of education, collaborative learning has emerged as a powerful tool for fostering student engagement, critical thinking, and communication skills. Flexible grouping, a key strategy within differentiated instruction, takes collaborative learning to the next level by strategically grouping students based on their individual needs, strengths, and learning styles.

This approach not only maximizes the benefits of collaboration but also ensures that all students are challenged and supported in their learning journey.

Flexible grouping moves away from the traditional practice of static, ability-based grouping, where students are placed in fixed groups for extended periods. Instead, it embraces a more dynamic and fluid approach, where groups are formed and re-formed based on specific learning objectives, tasks, or projects. This allows for greater flexibility in tailoring instruction to meet the diverse needs of all learners.

One of the primary benefits of flexible grouping is that it promotes a more inclusive learning environment. By grouping students with varying abilities, interests, and backgrounds, it creates opportunities for peer-to-peer learning and support.

Students who may struggle in a traditional classroom setting can benefit from working alongside more advanced peers, while those who are more advanced can deepen their understanding by explaining concepts to others.

Flexible grouping also encourages students to develop essential 21st-century skills, such as communication, collaboration, and problem-solving. When working in groups, students learn to share ideas, negotiate, compromise, and resolve conflicts.

They also learn to leverage each other's strengths, compensate for each other's weaknesses, and work together towards a common goal. These skills are not only valuable in the academic realm but also essential for success in the workplace and beyond.

There are various strategies for implementing flexible grouping in the classroom. One common approach is ability grouping, where students are grouped based on their readiness levels. This allows teachers to provide targeted instruction and support to each group, ensuring that all students are challenged and engaged.

However, it's important to avoid labeling students based on ability and to provide opportunities for them to move between groups as their skills develop.

Another strategy is interest grouping, where students are grouped based on their shared interests or passions. This can be particularly effective in project-based learning environments, where students are given the autonomy to choose topics that resonate with them. Interest grouping not only increases student engagement but also allows them to explore their passions in greater depth.

Mixed-ability grouping is another approach that can be beneficial. By intentionally grouping students with varying abilities, teachers can create opportunities for peer tutoring and mentoring. This can be particularly helpful for students who struggle with certain concepts, as they can receive support from their peers in a more informal and collaborative setting.

Regardless of the specific grouping strategy employed, it's important to establish clear expectations and guidelines for collaborative work. This includes defining roles and responsibilities, setting ground rules for communication and conflict resolution, and providing regular feedback and support.

It's also crucial to ensure that all students have the opportunity to contribute to the group's success, regardless of their individual abilities or learning styles.

Technology can also play a valuable role in facilitating flexible grouping. Online platforms and collaborative tools can enable students to work together seamlessly, regardless of their physical location. They can also provide teachers with real-time data on student progress and engagement, allowing them to adjust groups and provide targeted support as needed.

In conclusion, flexible grouping is a powerful strategy for enhancing collaborative learning and fostering a more inclusive and engaging classroom environment.

By strategically grouping students based on their individual needs, strengths, and interests, teachers can maximize the benefits of collaboration, promote the development of essential 21st-century skills, and ensure that all students are challenged and supported in their learning journey. As educators continue to explore innovative ways to personalize learning and meet the diverse needs of their students, flexible grouping will undoubtedly remain a valuable tool in their arsenal.

ᐯᐯᐯ

Technology is not a substitute for good teaching; it's a toolbox that expands our possibilities. Differentiated technology is the craftsman, selecting the right tools for each task and adapting them to individual needs. Let's harness the power of technology to enhance learning for all.

NINE

TIERED INSTRUCTION: MEETING DIVERSE READINESS LEVELS

In the mosaic of a classroom, students arrive with diverse backgrounds, experiences, and levels of prior knowledge. Tiered instruction, a cornerstone of differentiated instruction, embraces this diversity by providing a multi-layered approach to teaching that caters to the varying readiness levels of all learners. It is a strategic framework that empowers educators to challenge high achievers, support struggling learners, and engage those in between, ensuring that every student is appropriately challenged and supported to reach their full potential.

At its essence, tiered instruction recognizes that a one-size-fits-all approach to curriculum falls short in meeting the diverse needs of today's classrooms. It acknowledges that students learn at different paces, have varying levels of prior knowledge, and possess unique strengths and weaknesses. Tiered instruction allows teachers to differentiate their instruction by creating multiple pathways to learning, each tailored to a specific level of readiness.

The foundation of tiered instruction lies in the concept of the Zone of Proximal Development (ZPD), a theory developed by psychologist Lev Vygotsky. The ZPD is the sweet spot between what a learner can do independently and what they can achieve with guidance and support. Tiered instruction aims to place each student in their ZPD, providing them with tasks and activities that are challenging enough to promote growth but not so difficult that they become discouraged.

To implement tiered instruction effectively, teachers first need to assess their students' readiness levels. This can be done through pre-assessments, formative assessments, and observations. Once readiness levels are determined, teachers can design tiered assignments that offer varying levels of complexity and challenge.

A typical tiered assignment might have three tiers:

Tier 1. This tier is designed for students who are below grade level or who have significant gaps in their knowledge. It focuses on foundational skills and concepts, providing ample scaffolding and support. Tasks in this tier are typically more concrete and structured, with clear expectations and step-by-step instructions.

Tier 2. This tier is designed for students who are at grade level or slightly above. It focuses on applying and extending knowledge, requiring students to demonstrate understanding through analysis, synthesis, and evaluation. Tasks in this tier are typically more open-ended and require greater independence and critical thinking.

Tier 3. This tier is designed for students who are well above grade level or who are ready for more advanced challenges. It focuses on higher-order thinking skills, such as synthesis, evaluation, and creation. Tasks in this tier are typically more complex and require students to apply their knowledge in novel and creative ways.

The tiers in a tiered assignment are not fixed; students can move between tiers as their skills and understanding evolve. This flexibility is a key advantage of tiered instruction, as it allows teachers to respond to individual student needs in real time.

Tiered instruction can be applied to a variety of subjects and topics. In math, for example, a tiered assignment on fractions might include tasks ranging from basic fraction identification and representation (Tier 1) to solving complex word problems involving fractions (Tier 3). In a social studies unit on ancient civilizations, students might be asked to create a timeline of key events (Tier 1), analyze the impact of geography on cultural development (Tier 2), or design a hypothetical ancient civilization based on specific criteria (Tier 3).

The benefits of tiered instruction are numerous. For students, it provides a more personalized learning experience that caters to their individual needs and abilities. It helps to build confidence and motivation by allowing students to work at a level that is challenging but achievable. It also promotes critical thinking and problem-solving skills by requiring students to apply their knowledge in different ways.

For teachers, tiered instruction provides a framework for differentiating instruction and meeting the diverse needs of their students. It allows them to monitor student progress more effectively and provide targeted support to those who need it. It also helps to create a more inclusive classroom environment where all students feel valued and challenged.

In conclusion, tiered instruction is a powerful tool that can transform classrooms into vibrant learning communities where every student can thrive. By providing multiple pathways to learning, it ensures that all students are appropriately challenged and supported, regardless of their starting point. As educators continue to explore innovative ways to personalize learning and meet the diverse needs of their students, tiered instruction will undoubtedly remain a valuable strategy in their toolkit.

ppp

Collaboration is not a competition; it's a symphony of diverse voices. Differentiated collaboration is the conductor, orchestrating a harmonious blend of talents and perspectives. Let's create a classroom where every student's voice contributes to the melody of learning.

TEN

CHOICE BOARDS: EMPOWERING STUDENT CHOICE AND OWNERSHIP

In the vibrant tapestry of a differentiated classroom, choice boards emerge as a powerful tool for empowering students and fostering a sense of ownership over their learning journey. Like a buffet of educational options, choice boards present learners with a variety of engaging activities and assignments, allowing them to select those that align with their individual interests, strengths, and learning styles. This student-centered approach not only enhances motivation and engagement but also cultivates critical thinking, decision-making, and self-regulation skills that are essential for lifelong learning.

At their core, choice boards are visual organizers that display a range of learning activities or tasks related to a specific topic or unit of study. These boards typically offer a variety of options, catering to different learning styles and preferences. For example, a choice board for a unit on the solar system might include options such as writing a research paper on a chosen planet, creating a model of the solar system, composing a song about the planets, or designing an interactive presentation. This diverse array of options empowers students to choose activities that resonate with them, sparking their curiosity and igniting their passion for learning.

One of the key benefits of choice boards is that they promote student autonomy and agency. By allowing students to make choices about their learning, educators send a powerful message: their voices matter, their opinions are valued, and they are capable of taking charge of their education. This sense of ownership not only enhances student engagement but also fosters a deeper understanding of the material. When students are invested in their learning, they are more likely to actively participate, ask questions, and seek out additional information.

Choice boards also cater to diverse learning styles and preferences. Not all students learn best through traditional lectures and worksheets. Some thrive with hands-on activities, while others prefer visual or auditory learning. Choice boards offer a buffet of options, allowing students to select activities that align with their individual strengths and preferences. This not only maximizes their learning potential but also helps them develop a greater awareness of their own learning styles.

Furthermore, choice boards can be differentiated to meet the diverse needs of learners at different levels of readiness. By offering a variety of tasks with varying levels of complexity, teachers can ensure that all students are challenged and supported. For instance, a choice board for a math unit on fractions might include options for students who are just beginning to grasp the concept, as well as more challenging options for those who are ready to apply their knowledge in more complex ways.

In addition to promoting student autonomy and catering to diverse learning styles, choice boards can also foster collaboration and communication skills. Students can work together to complete tasks, share their insights and perspectives, and learn from each other. This collaborative aspect not only enhances the learning experience but also prepares students for the collaborative nature of the modern workplace.

Creating effective choice boards requires careful planning and consideration. Teachers need to select activities that align with the learning objectives, offer a variety of options, and provide clear instructions and expectations. It's also important to provide regular feedback and support to students as they work on their chosen activities.

Technology can be a valuable tool for creating and implementing choice boards. Online platforms and learning management systems offer a variety of templates and resources for designing engaging and interactive choice boards. They can also facilitate collaboration and communication between students and teachers, making it easier to provide feedback and support.

In conclusion, choice boards are a versatile and powerful tool for empowering students and fostering a sense of ownership over their learning. By offering a variety of engaging activities and assignments, catering to diverse learning styles, and promoting student autonomy, choice boards create a more inclusive and student-centered learning environment. As educators continue to seek innovative ways to personalize learning and meet the diverse needs of their students, choice boards will undoubtedly remain a valuable strategy in their toolkit.

ppp

The learning environment is not just a physical space; it's an emotional landscape. Differentiated environments are sanctuaries, nurturing a sense of belonging, safety, and respect. Let's create classrooms where every student feels valued and empowered.

ELEVEN

Learning Contracts: Individualizing Learning Goals

In the ever-evolving landscape of education, where personalized learning is gaining increasing prominence, learning contracts emerge as a powerful tool for individualizing learning goals and empowering students to take ownership of their educational journey. Unlike traditional, one-size-fits-all approaches, learning contracts foster a student-centered environment where learners actively participate in setting their own objectives, designing their learning paths, and evaluating their progress. This collaborative and personalized approach not only enhances student engagement and motivation but also cultivates essential skills such as goal setting, time management, self-regulation, and self-assessment.

At their core, learning contracts are agreements between a student and a teacher that outline specific learning goals, strategies, resources, and assessment criteria. These contracts are not rigid prescriptions but rather flexible frameworks that can be tailored to each student's individual needs, interests, and learning styles. They provide a roadmap for learning, allowing students to take charge of their education and progress at their own pace.

The process of creating a learning contract begins with a collaborative discussion between the student and teacher. Together, they identify the student's learning goals, which can be based on academic standards, personal interests, or career aspirations. These goals should be specific, measurable, achievable, relevant, and time-bound (SMART). For example, a student's learning goal might be to improve their writing skills, master a particular concept in math, or explore a specific topic in history.

Once the learning goals are established, the student and teacher work together to develop a plan of action. This plan outlines the specific steps the student will take to achieve their goals, the resources they will use, and the timeline for completion. The plan may also include checkpoints for monitoring progress and providing feedback.

Learning contracts can take various forms, from simple written agreements to more elaborate multimedia presentations. The key is that they are personalized to each student, reflecting their unique learning needs and preferences. Some students may prefer to work independently, while others may thrive in collaborative settings. Some may prefer to complete tasks online, while others may prefer traditional pen-and-paper activities. Learning contracts can accommodate these diverse preferences, providing students with the flexibility and autonomy to learn in ways that work best for them.

The benefits of learning contracts extend far beyond simply individualizing learning goals. They also foster a sense of ownership and responsibility among students. When learners are actively involved in setting their own goals and designing their learning paths, they are more likely to be invested in their education and motivated to succeed. This sense of ownership can lead to increased engagement, deeper understanding, and better academic performance.

Learning contracts also promote the development of essential life skills. By setting goals, planning their time, monitoring their progress, and evaluating their work, students learn to become self-directed learners. They develop the ability to set priorities, manage their time effectively, and take responsibility for their own success. These skills are not only valuable in the academic realm but also crucial for success in the workplace and in life.

Moreover, learning contracts can create a more collaborative and supportive learning environment. When students and teachers work together to set goals and create learning plans, it fosters a sense of partnership and mutual respect. Students feel heard and understood, while teachers gain valuable insights into their students' learning needs and preferences. This collaborative approach can lead to stronger relationships between students and teachers, increased trust, and a more positive learning experience for all.

While learning contracts offer numerous benefits, they are not without their challenges. They require a significant investment of time and effort on the part of both students and teachers. They also require a willingness to embrace flexibility and adapt to individual needs. However, the potential rewards of learning contracts far outweigh the challenges. By empowering students to take ownership of their learning, fostering essential life skills, and creating a more collaborative and supportive learning environment, learning contracts can truly transform the educational experience.

⮞⮞⮞

Learning is not a solitary pursuit; it's a journey best taken together. Differentiated grouping is the tour guide, creating diverse travel companions who learn and grow from each other. Let's build a classroom community where collaboration and support are the norm.

TWELVE

INTEREST-BASED LEARNING: ENGAGING STUDENT CURIOSITY

In the quest for educational excellence, educators are constantly seeking innovative approaches to ignite a passion for learning in their students. Interest-based learning, a student-centered approach that harnesses the power of curiosity and personal interests, has emerged as a transformative force in classrooms worldwide. By tapping into students' intrinsic motivation and allowing them to explore topics that genuinely captivate them, this approach not only enhances engagement and enjoyment but also cultivates deeper understanding, critical thinking, and a lifelong love of learning.

At its core, interest-based learning recognizes that students are not blank slates but rather individuals with unique passions, curiosities, and talents. By allowing students to pursue topics that spark their interest, educators tap into a wellspring of intrinsic motivation that fuels their desire to learn. This stands in stark contrast to traditional, teacher-centered approaches that often prioritize rote memorization and compliance with predetermined curricula, leaving little room for student agency or exploration.

Interest-based learning can take many forms, from independent projects and research to group collaborations and community-based learning experiences. The key is that students are given the autonomy to choose topics that resonate with them and to pursue those topics in ways that align with their individual learning styles and preferences. This might involve delving into a particular historical period, investigating a scientific phenomenon, creating a work of art, or designing a solution to a real-world problem.

The benefits of interest-based learning are numerous and far-reaching. First and foremost, it enhances student engagement and motivation. When students are genuinely interested in what they are learning, they are more likely to be attentive, participate actively, and persevere through challenges. This increased engagement not only leads to deeper understanding of the subject matter but also cultivates a sense of curiosity and wonder that extends beyond the classroom walls.

Interest-based learning also promotes the development of critical thinking skills. As students delve deeper into their chosen topics, they are encouraged to ask questions, analyze information, evaluate evidence, and draw their own conclusions. They learn to think critically and creatively, to challenge assumptions, and to consider multiple perspectives. These skills are essential for success in the 21st century, where information overload and rapid change require individuals to be adaptable, resourceful, and able to think for themselves.

Moreover, interest-based learning fosters a sense of ownership and agency among students. When learners are given the freedom to choose their own topics and pursue them in their own way, they develop a sense of responsibility for their learning. They become active participants in the educational process, setting goals, making decisions, and evaluating their progress. This sense of ownership not only enhances their academic performance but also prepares them for the challenges and opportunities of the real world.

Interest-based learning also has the potential to bridge the gap between school and the real world. By allowing students to explore topics that are relevant to their lives and communities, it helps them see the connections between what they learn in school and the world around them. This can be particularly powerful for students who may feel disengaged or alienated from traditional academic subjects.

Furthermore, interest-based learning can create a more inclusive and equitable learning environment. By valuing and celebrating students' diverse interests and talents, it sends a message that all learners are capable of success. It also provides opportunities for students to share their unique perspectives and experiences, enriching the learning experience for everyone involved.

While interest-based learning offers numerous benefits, it is not without its challenges. It requires a shift in mindset from traditional, teacher-centered approaches to a more student-centered approach. It also requires teachers to be flexible and adaptable, willing to let go of some control and trust students to take the lead in their learning. However, the potential rewards of interest-based learning far outweigh the challenges.

In conclusion, interest-based learning is a powerful approach that can transform classrooms into vibrant hubs of inquiry and discovery. By tapping into students' intrinsic motivation, fostering critical thinking, and promoting a sense of ownership and agency, it not only enhances academic achievement but also prepares students for success in the 21st century. As educators continue to seek innovative ways to engage and empower learners, interest-based learning will undoubtedly remain a vital tool in their arsenal.

❧❧❧

The curriculum is not a rigid set of rules; it's a flexible framework for exploration. Differentiated curriculum is the architect, designing learning experiences that cater to diverse interests and needs. Let's create classrooms where curiosity is ignited and passions are pursued.

THIRTEEN

UNIVERSAL DESIGN FOR LEARNING: CREATING ACCESSIBLE LESSONS

In the quest for educational equity, Universal Design for Learning (UDL) emerges as a beacon of inclusivity, illuminating a path towards creating accessible lessons that cater to the diverse needs of all learners. UDL is not merely a set of guidelines or accommodations; it is a transformative framework that shifts the paradigm of teaching and learning, ensuring that every student, regardless of their abilities, disabilities, or learning styles, has equal access to engaging and meaningful educational experiences.

At its core, UDL is rooted in the understanding that learners differ in the ways they perceive, process, and express information. It recognizes that traditional teaching methods, which often rely on a one-size-fits-all approach, can create barriers for students with diverse needs. UDL, on the other hand, advocates for a more flexible and adaptable approach, one that proactively anticipates and addresses these barriers by providing multiple means of representation, action and expression, and engagement.

The first principle of UDL, multiple means of representation, emphasizes the importance of presenting information in various formats to cater to different learning styles and preferences. This can involve using text, audio, visuals, and even hands-on activities to convey the same concept. For example, in a history lesson, a teacher might provide students with a textbook chapter, a documentary video, a collection of primary source documents, and a hands-on simulation of a historical event. By offering multiple ways to access the content, teachers ensure that all students can engage with the material in a way that makes sense to them.

The second principle, multiple means of action and expression, recognizes that learners differ in how they demonstrate their understanding. Some students may excel at writing essays, while others may prefer to create presentations, build models, or perform skits. UDL encourages teachers to provide a variety of assessment options, allowing students to showcase their learning in ways that align with their strengths and interests. This not only makes assessments more equitable but also encourages creativity and self-expression.

The third principle, multiple means of engagement, focuses on tapping into students' intrinsic motivation and fostering a love of learning. This can be achieved by offering choices, providing opportunities for collaboration, and connecting learning to real-world applications. For example, in a science class, students might be allowed to choose their research topics, work together on experiments, or apply their knowledge to solve a community problem. By engaging students in meaningful and relevant ways, teachers can spark their curiosity, inspire their creativity, and instill a lifelong passion for learning.

UDL is not just about accommodating students with disabilities;

it's about creating learning environments that are accessible and inclusive for all learners. It's about removing barriers to learning, whether they are physical, sensory, cognitive, or affective. For example, a classroom that is universally designed might have ramps for wheelchair access, adjustable lighting for students with visual sensitivities, and noise-canceling headphones for students who are easily distracted.

Technology can play a pivotal role in implementing UDL. Digital tools and platforms offer a wealth of resources for creating accessible and engaging learning experiences. For example, text-to-speech software can help students with reading difficulties access written materials, while online simulations and virtual labs can provide hands-on learning opportunities for students with physical disabilities.

UDL is not a one-size-fits-all solution; it's a framework that guides educators in creating flexible and adaptable learning environments that can meet the diverse needs of all learners. It requires ongoing reflection, collaboration, and a willingness to experiment with new approaches. However, the benefits of UDL are undeniable.

By embracing UDL, educators can create classrooms where all students feel valued, challenged, and supported. They can foster a love of learning that extends far beyond the classroom walls, equipping students with the skills and knowledge they need to succeed in the 21st century. As our understanding of learning and neuroscience continues to evolve, UDL will remain a critical tool for creating a more equitable and inclusive educational system.

ᕴᕴᕴ

Motivation is not an external reward; it's an internal fire that fuels learning. Differentiated motivation is the spark, igniting each student's unique passions and interests. Let's create classrooms where learning is a joy, not a chore.

FOURTEEN

TECHNOLOGY FOR DIFFERENTIATION: TOOLS AND RESOURCES

In the ever-evolving landscape of education, technology has emerged as a powerful ally for differentiated instruction, offering a vast array of tools and resources that empower educators to personalize learning experiences and cater to the diverse needs of their students. From adaptive learning platforms and assistive technologies to multimedia resources and collaboration tools, technology has the potential to transform the classroom into a dynamic and inclusive learning environment where every student can thrive.

Adaptive learning platforms are at the forefront of technology-driven differentiation. These platforms utilize sophisticated algorithms to assess students' individual strengths and weaknesses, tailoring the content, pace, and feedback of instruction to meet their specific needs. As students progress through the material, the platform continuously adapts to their performance, providing additional challenges or support as needed. This personalized approach ensures that all students are working at their optimal level, maximizing their learning potential.

Assistive technologies are another vital component of technology for differentiation. These tools are designed to help students with disabilities access and engage with the curriculum. For example, text-to-speech software can help students with reading difficulties, while screen magnifiers and alternative keyboards can assist students with visual or motor impairments. By leveraging assistive technologies, educators can create a more inclusive learning environment where all students have the opportunity to succeed.

Multimedia resources, such as videos, animations, and interactive simulations, can also play a crucial role in differentiated instruction. These resources can cater to different learning styles, providing visual and auditory learners with alternative ways to access and process information. They can also make complex concepts more accessible and engaging, sparking curiosity and fostering deeper understanding.

Collaboration tools, such as online discussion forums, shared documents, and video conferencing platforms, facilitate communication and collaboration among students, regardless of their physical location. This is particularly beneficial for students who may be unable to attend school due to illness or other circumstances. Collaboration tools also enable students to work together on projects, share ideas, and provide feedback to each other, fostering a sense of community and shared learning.

Gamification, the application of game-like elements to non-game contexts, can also be a powerful motivator for students. By incorporating points, badges, leaderboards, and other game mechanics into learning activities, educators can tap into students' intrinsic motivation and make learning more fun and engaging.

Gamification can also be used to differentiate instruction by providing different levels of challenge and rewards based on individual student needs.

Virtual reality (VR) and augmented reality (AR) are emerging technologies that have the potential to revolutionize differentiated instruction. These immersive technologies can create realistic simulations of real-world environments, allowing students to explore complex concepts in a safe and engaging way. For example, students might use VR to explore the human body, travel back in time to ancient civilizations, or simulate scientific experiments.

Data analytics and learning analytics are also playing an increasingly important role in differentiated instruction. These tools can provide educators with valuable insights into student learning patterns, preferences, and areas of need. By analyzing this data, teachers can identify students who may be struggling and provide targeted support. They can also use data to personalize instruction, tailoring assignments and activities to meet the specific needs of each student.

While technology offers immense potential for differentiation, it's important to use it thoughtfully and intentionally. Technology should not be seen as a replacement for good teaching but rather as a tool to enhance and support it. Educators need to be mindful of potential pitfalls, such as digital distractions and the digital divide, and ensure that all students have equal access to technology and the skills to use it effectively.

In conclusion, technology has become an indispensable tool for differentiating instruction, offering a wealth of resources that empower educators to personalize learning experiences and cater to the diverse needs of their students. From adaptive learning platforms and assistive technologies to multimedia resources, collaboration tools, gamification, VR/AR, and data analytics, technology has the potential to transform the classroom into a dynamic and inclusive learning environment where every student can thrive. As technology continues to evolve, educators who embrace its potential for differentiation will be well-positioned to create a more equitable and engaging educational experience for all.

❧❧❧

Feedback is not a criticism; it's a compass guiding students towards improvement. Differentiated feedback is the GPS, providing personalized directions for each learner's journey. Let's empower students to take ownership of their learning by providing them with specific and actionable feedback.

FIFTEEN

Chapter 15:
Missing

❦

Success is not a destination; it's a journey of continuous growth and improvement. Differentiated instruction is the roadmap, guiding each student towards their individual definition of success. Let's create classrooms where every student's journey is celebrated.

SIXTEEN

DIFFERENTIATING FOR ENGLISH LANGUAGE LEARNERS: SUPPORTING LANGUAGE ACQUISITION

In the vibrant tapestry of a modern classroom, English Language Learners (ELLs) bring a rich diversity of cultural backgrounds and linguistic experiences. These students are on a unique journey of language acquisition, navigating the complexities of a new language while simultaneously grappling with academic content. Differentiating instruction for ELLs is not merely an option; it is an imperative, a commitment to ensuring that these learners have equitable access to a high-quality education and the support they need to thrive academically and linguistically.

At its core, differentiating instruction for ELLs involves recognizing and valuing their linguistic diversity. It acknowledges that language acquisition is a complex and multifaceted process that varies for each individual. Some ELLs may have had prior exposure to English, while others may be encountering it for the first time. Some may be proficient in reading and writing but struggle with oral communication, while others may be the opposite. By understanding these individual differences, educators can tailor their instruction to meet the specific needs of each ELL student.

Differentiating content is a crucial aspect of supporting language acquisition for ELLs. This involves scaffolding complex texts and concepts, breaking them down into smaller, more manageable chunks, and providing ample visual aids and real-world examples to enhance comprehension. Pre-teaching key vocabulary and providing graphic organizers can also facilitate understanding. Moreover, offering texts at varying reading levels and allowing students to choose topics that interest them can further boost engagement and motivation.

Differentiating process for ELLs means providing multiple pathways for learning. This can involve incorporating a variety of instructional strategies, such as visual aids, hands-on activities, collaborative projects, and technology-based tools. For example, using videos with subtitles, interactive games, and online language practice platforms can provide ELLs with additional opportunities to practice and reinforce their language skills. Pairing ELLs with native English speakers for peer tutoring or collaborative projects can also be beneficial, fostering language exchange and cultural understanding.

Differentiating product for ELLs means offering a variety of assessment options that allow them to demonstrate their knowledge and skills in ways that are comfortable and accessible to them. This might involve allowing them to use their native language for certain tasks, providing sentence frames or graphic organizers to support written expression, or offering oral presentations or visual projects as alternatives to traditional written assessments.

Creating a supportive and inclusive classroom environment is paramount for ELLs. This involves fostering a sense of belonging and respect for cultural diversity, celebrating linguistic differences, and providing ample opportunities for students to share their backgrounds and experiences. Establishing a positive and welcoming classroom climate can help ELLs feel comfortable taking risks, asking questions, and participating in class discussions.

Scaffolding is a key strategy for differentiating instruction for ELLs. This involves providing temporary support, such as graphic organizers, sentence starters, or visual aids, to help students access and understand complex content. As students gain proficiency, the scaffolding can be gradually removed, allowing them to become more independent learners.

Building background knowledge is another essential aspect of supporting language acquisition for ELLs. Many ELLs may lack the cultural and contextual knowledge that native English speakers take for granted. Teachers can bridge this gap by providing explicit instruction on relevant cultural references, historical events, or social customs.

Differentiating instruction for ELLs also involves recognizing and addressing affective factors, such as anxiety and self-confidence. ELLs may feel self-conscious or hesitant to participate in class due to their limited language skills. Teachers can create a safe and supportive learning environment by encouraging risk-taking, providing positive feedback, and celebrating even small successes.

Technology can be a powerful tool for differentiating instruction for

ELLs. Language learning apps, online dictionaries, and translation tools can provide valuable support for language development. Interactive whiteboards, document cameras, and other multimedia tools can make lessons more engaging and accessible.

In conclusion, differentiating instruction for English Language Learners is a multifaceted approach that involves tailoring content, process, and product to meet their unique linguistic and cultural needs. By creating a supportive and inclusive classroom environment, scaffolding instruction, building background knowledge, and addressing affective factors, educators can empower ELLs to become confident and successful learners. Technology can also play a vital role in supporting language acquisition, providing ELLs with access to a wealth of resources and tools. Ultimately, differentiating instruction for ELLs is about recognizing and valuing their linguistic diversity, providing them with the support they need to thrive academically, and empowering them to become active and engaged participants in their learning journey.

ϸϸϸ

Learning is not about conformity; it's about embracing individual differences. Differentiated instruction is the kaleidoscope, revealing the beauty and complexity of each learner's unique perspective. Let's create classrooms where diversity is celebrated and every student feels valued.

SEVENTEEN

DIFFERENTIATING FOR GIFTED LEARNERS: NURTURING POTENTIAL

In the vibrant tapestry of a classroom, gifted learners are often like bright threads, their minds brimming with exceptional abilities and insatiable curiosity. These students possess a unique blend of advanced cognitive abilities, heightened creativity, and a voracious appetite for knowledge. However, their exceptional potential can easily be stifled in a traditional, one-size-fits-all educational setting. Differentiating for gifted learners is not merely an option; it is a necessity, a commitment to nurturing their intellectual, creative, and emotional growth, ensuring they reach their full potential and make meaningful contributions to society.

At its core, differentiating for gifted learners involves recognizing and valuing their unique strengths and needs. It acknowledges that these students often process information more quickly, grasp complex concepts with ease, and exhibit exceptional problem-solving skills. They may also possess a heightened sensitivity, a deep sense of justice, and a passion for exploring ideas in depth. Differentiated instruction for gifted learners aims to provide them with the challenges, enrichment, and support they need to flourish academically, creatively, and emotionally.

Differentiation for gifted learners can take many forms. One approach is acceleration, which involves allowing students to move through the curriculum at a faster pace or to skip grades altogether. This can be particularly beneficial for students who are significantly ahead of their peers in certain subjects. Acceleration can prevent boredom, frustration, and underachievement, providing gifted learners with the opportunity to explore more advanced topics and reach their full potential.

Another approach is enrichment, which involves providing students with opportunities to delve deeper into their areas of interest and explore complex ideas beyond the standard curriculum. This can be achieved through a variety of activities, such as independent research projects, participation in academic competitions, mentorship programs, and summer enrichment programs. Enrichment can help gifted learners develop their passions, broaden their knowledge, and cultivate their creativity.

Differentiation can also involve grouping gifted learners together for certain activities or subjects. This allows them to interact with intellectual peers, share ideas, and engage in stimulating discussions. It can also provide them with the opportunity to work on more challenging projects and tackle complex problems collaboratively.

In addition to academic challenges, it is important to provide opportunities for gifted learners to develop their creative and leadership potential. This can be achieved through activities such as creative writing workshops, debate clubs, student government, and community service projects. By encouraging them to explore their passions and express themselves creatively, educators can help gifted learners develop a sense of purpose and make meaningful contributions to society.

Creating a supportive and inclusive classroom environment is essential for gifted learners. This involves fostering a culture of respect for individual differences, celebrating diversity, and encouraging intellectual risk-taking. Teachers should create a safe space where gifted learners feel comfortable asking questions, challenging assumptions, and expressing their unique perspectives.

Technology can also play a vital role in differentiating for gifted learners. Online learning platforms, virtual reality simulations, and educational games can provide them with access to a wealth of resources and opportunities for independent learning. They can also connect with other gifted learners from around the world, forming virtual communities where they can share ideas, collaborate on projects, and find support and inspiration.

Assessment for gifted learners should focus on growth and mastery rather than simply measuring achievement. This can involve using a variety of assessment tools, such as portfolios, performance tasks, and self-assessments, that allow students to demonstrate their understanding in multiple ways. It is also important to provide gifted learners with regular feedback that is specific, actionable, and focused on their strengths and areas for growth.

In conclusion, differentiating for gifted learners is a multifaceted approach that involves providing them with the challenges, enrichment, and support they need to thrive academically, creatively, and emotionally. By accelerating their learning, enriching their experiences, fostering their creativity, and creating a supportive and inclusive classroom environment, educators can unlock the full potential of these exceptional learners and prepare them to become the leaders, innovators, and problem-solvers of tomorrow.

ᏫᏫᏫ

The teacher is not a sage on the stage; they are a guide on the side. Differentiated instruction empowers teachers to become facilitators, mentors, and co-learners. Let's create classrooms where collaboration and shared discovery are the norm.

EIGHTEEN

ASSESSMENT FOR DIFFERENTIATION: MONITORING STUDENT PROGRESS

In the dynamic landscape of differentiated instruction, assessment plays a pivotal role in monitoring student progress, informing instructional decisions, and ensuring that every learner receives the tailored support and challenges they need to thrive. It is not merely a summative evaluation of learning but an ongoing, formative process that guides teachers in adapting their practices to meet the diverse needs of their students.

Assessment for differentiation goes beyond simply measuring student achievement against standardized benchmarks. It encompasses a wide range of tools and techniques designed to gather a holistic understanding of each student's strengths, weaknesses, learning styles, and interests. This comprehensive understanding serves as the foundation for tailoring instruction, ensuring that every student is working within their zone of proximal development, where they are challenged but not overwhelmed.

Formative assessment is a cornerstone of assessment for differentiation. Unlike summative assessments, which evaluate learning at the end of a unit or course, formative assessments are ongoing, embedded within the instructional process. They provide teachers with real-time feedback on student learning, allowing them to make adjustments to their instruction as needed. This might involve providing additional support to students who are struggling, offering enrichment activities to those who are ahead, or adjusting the pace or content of instruction to better meet the needs of the class.

Formative assessments can take many forms, such as observations, questioning, exit tickets, quick quizzes, and self-assessments. They are not meant to be graded but rather to provide information that can inform instructional decisions. For example, a teacher might use observations to gauge student engagement during a lesson, ask probing questions to assess their understanding of a concept, or have students complete exit tickets to summarize their key takeaways.

Another key aspect of assessment for differentiation is the use of multiple assessment modalities. This means offering students a variety of ways to demonstrate their learning, such as written assignments, oral presentations, visual projects, or performance-based assessments. This allows students to showcase their knowledge and skills in ways that align with their strengths and interests, ensuring that all learners have a fair and equitable opportunity to succeed.

Portfolios are another valuable tool for assessment in a differentiated classroom. They are collections of student work that showcase their progress over time. Portfolios can include a variety of artifacts, such as essays, projects, reflections, and self-assessments. They provide a more comprehensive picture of student learning than traditional tests and can be used to identify patterns of growth and areas for improvement.

Self-assessment is a crucial component of assessment for differentiation. When students are given the opportunity to reflect on their own learning, they develop metacognitive skills, such as self-awareness, self-regulation, and goal setting. Self-assessment can take many forms, such as journal entries, checklists, or rubrics. By engaging in self-assessment, students become active participants in their learning journey, taking ownership of their progress and identifying areas where they need additional support.

Technology can also play a significant role in assessment for differentiation. Digital tools and platforms can streamline the assessment process, automate data collection and analysis, and provide personalized feedback to students. They can also offer a wider range of assessment options, such as interactive quizzes, multimedia presentations, and virtual simulations.

Data-driven decision-making is another essential aspect of assessment for differentiation. By collecting and analyzing data from various assessments, teachers can gain valuable insights into student learning patterns, preferences, and areas of need. This data can then be used to inform instructional decisions, such as grouping students for differentiated activities, selecting appropriate materials and resources, and tailoring assessments to meet individual needs.

In conclusion, assessment for differentiation is a multifaceted process that plays a crucial role in monitoring student progress and ensuring that every learner receives the tailored support and challenges they need to succeed. By embracing formative assessment, multiple assessment modalities, portfolios, self-assessment, and technology, educators can create a more equitable and inclusive learning environment where all students have the opportunity to reach their full potential.

❧❧❧

Every child is a seed with the potential to grow into a magnificent tree. Differentiated instruction is the fertile soil, providing the nutrients and support each seed needs to flourish. Let's cultivate a learning environment where every child reaches their full potential.

NINETEEN

OVERCOMING CHALLENGES: STRATEGIES FOR SUCCESSFUL IMPLEMENTATION

Differentiated instruction, while promising a more equitable and engaging learning environment, is not without its challenges. These obstacles can range from practical concerns like time management and resource constraints to more complex issues like changing ingrained teaching habits and managing diverse student needs. However, with thoughtful planning, strategic implementation, and a commitment to growth, educators can overcome these challenges and successfully implement differentiated instruction in their classrooms.

One of the most common challenges in implementing differentiated instruction is the perceived lack of time. Teachers often feel overwhelmed by the demands of their daily schedules, leaving little room for the additional planning and preparation required for differentiated lessons. However, it's important to remember that differentiation doesn't necessarily mean creating entirely separate lessons for each student. Instead, it involves adapting existing lessons and materials to meet diverse needs. By incorporating flexible grouping, tiered activities, and a variety of assessment options, teachers can differentiate their instruction without sacrificing valuable time.

Another challenge is the availability of resources. While differentiated instruction doesn't require a vast array of expensive materials, it does require access to a variety of resources to cater to different learning styles and preferences. Teachers can overcome this challenge by seeking out free or low-cost resources online, collaborating with colleagues to share materials, and utilizing technology to create digital resources. They can also leverage the strengths of their students by encouraging them to create their own learning materials or share their knowledge and expertise with their peers.

Changing ingrained teaching habits can also be a significant hurdle for educators. Many teachers have been trained in traditional, teacher-centered approaches and may feel uncomfortable with the shift towards a more student-centered, differentiated approach. Overcoming this challenge requires a willingness to learn and grow, as well as a commitment to professional development. Teachers can participate in workshops and training sessions on differentiated instruction, read relevant books and articles, and collaborate with colleagues who are already successfully implementing this approach.

Managing diverse student needs can also be a complex challenge. Differentiated instruction requires teachers to understand and address the unique needs of each student, which can be a daunting task in a large classroom. However, by using a variety of assessment tools and techniques, teachers can gather information about students' learning styles, interests, and readiness levels. This information can then be used to create differentiated learning plans that cater to individual needs. Technology can also be a valuable tool in this regard, providing teachers with personalized learning platforms and data analytics that can help them track student progress and identify areas where they need additional support.

Another challenge is ensuring that all students are challenged and supported appropriately. Differentiated instruction is not about lowering standards or giving some students an easier path to success. It's about providing all students with the opportunities and resources they need to reach their full potential. This requires teachers to have high expectations for all learners, while also recognizing and addressing their individual needs. It also requires a willingness to experiment with different approaches and adapt as needed.

Building a supportive classroom culture is also crucial for the successful implementation of differentiated instruction. Students need to feel safe and respected in order to take risks, express their opinions, and collaborate with their peers. Teachers can foster a supportive classroom culture by establishing clear expectations, promoting positive communication, and celebrating diversity. They can also create opportunities for students to share their ideas, work together on projects, and learn from each other.

Parental involvement can also be a challenge in implementing differentiated instruction. Some parents may be unfamiliar with this approach and may have concerns about how it will impact their child's learning. Teachers can address this challenge by communicating openly and transparently with parents, explaining the benefits of differentiated instruction and how it works. They can also invite parents to participate in their child's learning by providing them with resources and strategies for supporting their child at home.

In conclusion, while differentiated instruction presents several challenges, these obstacles can be overcome with careful planning, strategic implementation, and a commitment to growth. By addressing time constraints, resource limitations, changing teaching habits, managing diverse student needs, ensuring appropriate challenge and support, building a supportive classroom culture, and involving parents, educators can successfully implement differentiated instruction and create a more equitable and engaging learning environment for all students.

ᴘᴘᴘ

Learning is not a competition; it's a collaboration between students, teachers, and the curriculum. Differentiated instruction is the bridge, connecting these three pillars to create a harmonious learning experience. Let's build classrooms where everyone works together to achieve success.

Building a Differentiated Classroom Community: Fostering Collaboration and Growth

In the intricate dance of education, a classroom is not merely a space where knowledge is imparted; it is a dynamic community where learners and educators come together to explore, discover, and grow. Building a differentiated classroom community is an art that goes beyond individual learning needs and delves into the intricate web of social and emotional connections that underpin a thriving educational environment.

It is a conscious effort to create a space where diversity is celebrated, collaboration is fostered, and every student feels valued, supported, and empowered to reach their full potential.

At its core, a differentiated classroom community embraces the uniqueness of each learner. It recognizes that students come from diverse backgrounds, possess varied strengths and challenges, and learn in different ways. This diversity, far from being a hurdle, is viewed as an asset, a source of richness and strength that can enrich the learning experience for everyone involved.

Creating a differentiated classroom community begins with fostering a sense of belonging. Students need to feel safe, respected, and valued for who they are. This can be achieved through simple but powerful gestures, such as greeting each student by name, acknowledging their contributions, and creating opportunities for them to share their experiences and perspectives.

Building relationships based on trust and mutual respect is essential, as it allows students to feel comfortable taking risks, asking questions, and seeking help when needed.

Collaboration lies at the heart of a differentiated classroom community. It is not just about working together on tasks; it's about creating a culture of shared learning and mutual support. Students learn to appreciate each other's strengths, learn from each other's mistakes, and work together to achieve common goals.

Collaborative learning can take many forms, such as group projects, peer tutoring, jigsaw activities, and think-pair-share discussions. These activities not only enhance learning but also foster social and emotional skills such as communication, empathy, and cooperation.

Growth is another key pillar of a differentiated classroom community. It is a space where students are encouraged to stretch their intellectual boundaries, explore new ideas, and challenge themselves. This can be achieved through a variety of differentiated instructional strategies, such as tiered assignments, learning contracts, and choice boards.

These strategies allow students to learn at their own pace, pursue their interests, and demonstrate their learning in ways that align with their strengths.

A differentiated classroom community is also characterized by a growth mindset, a belief that intelligence and abilities can be developed through effort and perseverance. This mindset encourages students to embrace challenges, learn from mistakes, and persist in the face of setbacks. It creates a culture of resilience and optimism, where students are not afraid to take risks and try new things.

Technology can play a significant role in building a differentiated classroom community. Digital tools and platforms can facilitate communication and collaboration among students, even when they are not physically present in the same space. Online forums, discussion boards, and collaborative documents can create virtual spaces for students to share ideas, provide feedback, and work together on projects.

Assessment in a differentiated classroom community is not just about measuring individual achievement; it's also about celebrating collective growth.

By focusing on formative assessment, teachers can provide students with timely feedback that helps them identify their strengths and areas for improvement. Peer assessment and self-assessment can also be valuable tools for fostering a sense of shared responsibility for learning.

Building a differentiated classroom community is an ongoing

process that requires commitment, creativity, and a willingness to adapt. It involves cultivating a positive and inclusive classroom culture, fostering collaboration and growth, and using technology to enhance learning experiences.

When done effectively, a differentiated classroom community can empower students to become lifelong learners who are not only academically successful but also compassionate, resilient, and engaged citizens of the world.

ppp

Education is not about filling a bucket; it's about lighting a fire. Differentiated instruction is the match, igniting a passion for learning that burns brightly throughout a student's life. Let's create classrooms where the fire of learning is never extinguished.

TWENTY-ONE
SUMMARY

Differentiating instruction is a dynamic, student-centered approach that tailors teaching to the diverse needs of all learners. It recognizes that students are not uniform but unique individuals with varying strengths, challenges, interests, and learning styles. By acknowledging and embracing this diversity, differentiated instruction empowers educators to create inclusive and engaging learning environments where every student can thrive.

The foundation of differentiated instruction lies in understanding the students. Through a combination of formal and informal assessments, observations, conversations, and analysis of student work, teachers gain valuable insights into each learner's readiness levels, learning profiles, and interests. This understanding allows teachers to tailor their instruction to meet the specific needs of each student, providing them with the appropriate level of challenge and support.

Differentiating content is a key aspect of this approach. It involves adjusting the complexity and depth of the material to match individual needs. Tiered instruction, flexible grouping, and choice boards are effective strategies for differentiating content, allowing students to work at a level that is both challenging and attainable. Technology can also play a vital role in providing personalized learning experiences.

Differentiating process refers to adapting how students learn. Recognizing that students learn in different ways, teachers can offer a variety of instructional strategies, such as hands-on activities, visual aids, graphic organizers, and collaborative learning experiences. Scaffolding and the use of technology can further enhance the learning process, catering to diverse learning styles and preferences.

Differentiating product means providing students with multiple ways to demonstrate their learning. This can involve allowing students to choose from various formats, such as written assignments, oral presentations, visual projects, or artistic creations. Tiered assignments and incorporating student interests can further personalize the learning experience.

The learning environment plays a crucial role in differentiated instruction. Creating a supportive and inclusive classroom involves considering the physical layout, classroom culture, and instructional practices. Flexible seating arrangements, visually stimulating displays, and a positive classroom culture that values diversity and collaboration are all essential components of a differentiated learning environment.

Flexible grouping is another key strategy for differentiated instruction. By strategically grouping students based on their readiness levels, interests, or learning styles, teachers can maximize the benefits of collaboration and peer-to-peer learning. Different grouping strategies, such as ability grouping, interest grouping, and mixed-ability grouping, can be used to cater to diverse needs.

Tiered instruction is a powerful tool for meeting the diverse readiness levels of students. By creating multiple tiers of instruction, each with varying levels of complexity and challenge, teachers can ensure that all students are appropriately challenged and supported. The flexibility of tiered instruction allows students to move between tiers as their skills and understanding evolve.

Choice boards empower students by giving them a voice in their learning journey. By offering a variety of learning activities and allowing students to choose those that align with their interests and learning styles, teachers can foster a sense of ownership and engagement. Choice boards can also be differentiated to cater to different readiness levels.

Learning contracts are another way to personalize learning goals. These agreements between students and teachers outline specific learning objectives, strategies, resources, and assessment criteria. By actively participating in setting their own goals and designing their learning paths, students develop a sense of ownership and responsibility for their learning.

Interest-based learning harnesses the power of curiosity to ignite a passion for learning. By allowing students to explore topics that genuinely captivate them, teachers can tap into a wellspring of intrinsic motivation that fuels their desire to learn. Interest-based learning promotes deeper understanding, critical thinking, and a lifelong love of learning.

Universal Design for Learning (UDL) is a framework that guides educators in creating accessible lessons that cater to the diverse needs of all learners. By providing multiple means of representation, action and expression, and engagement, UDL ensures that every student has equal access to engaging and meaningful educational experiences.

Technology plays a crucial role in differentiated instruction. Adaptive learning platforms, assistive technologies, multimedia resources, collaboration tools, gamification, virtual reality, and data analytics can all be leveraged to personalize learning experiences, cater to diverse learning styles, and provide targeted support.

Differentiating for English Language Learners (ELLs) involves tailoring content, process, and product to meet their unique linguistic and cultural needs. Strategies such as scaffolding, building background knowledge, and offering a variety of assessment options can empower ELLs to become confident and successful learners.

Differentiating for gifted learners involves providing them with the challenges, enrichment, and support they need to reach their full potential. Acceleration, enrichment activities, grouping with intellectual peers, and opportunities for creative expression are all important aspects of differentiating for gifted learners.

Assessment for differentiation is an ongoing, formative process that guides instructional decisions. By using a variety of assessment tools and techniques, teachers can gather a holistic understanding of each student's strengths, weaknesses, learning styles, and interests. This information can then be used to tailor instruction, provide targeted support, and ensure that all students are appropriately challenged and engaged.

Implementing differentiated instruction can present challenges, such as time constraints, limited resources, and the need to change ingrained teaching habits. However, with careful planning, strategic implementation, and a commitment to growth, educators can overcome these challenges and create a thriving differentiated classroom community.

Building a differentiated classroom community involves fostering a sense of belonging, encouraging collaboration, and promoting growth. It involves creating a safe and inclusive space where students feel valued, respected, and empowered to learn. By embracing diversity, celebrating individual differences, and providing personalized learning experiences, educators can create a classroom community where every student can thrive.

❦❦❦

Citation And References

This book represents the culmination of extensive research and meticulous analysis, incorporating a diverse range of sources, including numerous books, scholarly studies, and personal experiences. Additionally, I have scoured various websites to gather relevant information and data essential for the compilation of this work. I have taken every precaution to ensure the accuracy of the information presented and have diligently cited all sources to acknowledge their contributions.

Despite these efforts, the possibility of inadvertent errors remains. I deeply value the insights of my readers and appreciate any feedback that can help identify and rectify such inaccuracies. I encourage you to bring any discrepancies to my attention.

Your feedback is not only welcome but crucial, as it will aid in correcting current editions and enhancing the content of future ones. I am committed to maintaining the highest standards of accuracy and reliability in my work and thank you for your support and understanding.

Additionally, I firmly uphold the principle of freedom of speech and expression as guaranteed under Article 19(1)(a) of the Constitution of India, and I respect the diverse viewpoints and expressions of all readers.

ᐞᐞᐞ

Other Books Of The Author

1. Empowering Minds: A Journey into Women's Self-Discovery and Power
2. The Dynamics of Motivation: Catalyzing Thought into Action
3. Meditation and Mental Well Being: The Path to Inner Peace and Clarity
4. The Psychology of Child Education: Nurturing Future Generations
5. Ethical Enlightenment: A Modern Guide to Living with Integrity
6. Voices of Empowerment: Stories of Women Rising Against Odds
7. Social Psychology in Everyday Life: Understanding Human Connections
8. The Essence of Motivational Speaking: Inspiring Change in Others
9. Balancing Acts: Women, Work, and the Will to Lead
10. Guiding with Grace: Raising Children with Compassion and Awareness
11. The Power of Positive Aging: Embracing Life After Fifty
12. Building Resilient Communities: Social Work in Action
13. The Ethical Educator: Principles for Teaching and Learning
14. From Insight to Impact: Social Psychology for a Better World
15. The Ethics of Empathy: A Guide to Ethical Living
16. The Science of Empowering the Self: Navigating Life's Challenges with Psychological Wisdom
17. The Mindful Conscious Leader: Meditation Techniques for Modern Management
18. Pioneering Spirit: Women's Pathways to Leadership and Empowerment
19. Feeling to Healing: The Role of Emotional Intelligence in Child Development
20. Transformative Talks and Words of Inspiration: Insights into Motivational Oratory

in a Complex World

46. Secret of Solopreneur's Odyssey: Navigating the Path to Self-Employment
47. Exploring Tapestry of Peace: Global Perspectives on Harmony
48. The Art and Actions of Connection: Mastering Communication for Impact
49. She Governs and at the Helm: Strategies for Political Empowerment
50. Rising Above and Rising with Grace: A Woman's Roadmap to Career Mastery
51. The Effect of Networking & Connectedness: Building Strategic Alliances for Women
52. Beyond his Barriers: Women Thriving in Male-Dominated Fields
53. Secret of Inner Compass: Navigating Life with Intuition
54. Creative & Pro-Active Muses: A Celebration of Women in the Arts
55. Unburdened: The Art of Releasing the Past
56. Amplified Voices: Speeches of Women that Astonished the World
57. Secret of Manifesting Dreams: A Woman's Guide to Intentional Living
58. Ethics and Value Based Education: Reimagining Japan's School System
59. The Moral Compass Curriculum: A Holistic Approach
60. Tech with Heart: Integrating Ethics into Digital Learning
61. Honoring Virtue: Recognizing Ethical Excellence in Education
62. Raising Good Humans: A Guide to Character Development
63. The Spark Within: Nurturing Creativity in Children
64. The Teenager Whisperer: Navigating Adolescence with Grace
65. Igniting a Passion for Learning: Inspiring Lifelong Curiosity
66. The Habit Lab: Cultivating Positive Behaviors in Children
67. Seeds of Empathy: Fostering Compassion in Young Hearts
68. The Reading Revolution: Inspiring a Love of Books in Children
69. The Learning Brain: Unlocking the Secrets of Student Success
70. Teaching for All: Differentiated Instruction Strategies
71. The Time Alchemist: Mastering Time Management for Peak Performance

Bhajan

101. Pilgrimage of the Soul: Spiritual Journeys in India

❧❧❧

Contact

Dr. Minakshi Bansal
Social Activist
Ahmedabad, Gujarat, Bharat
minakshiindiag20@yahoo.com

⊳⊳⊳

|| LOKAHA SAMASTHAHA SUKHINO BHAVANTU ||